GRAPHIC SCIENCE

EXPLORING

ECOSYSTEMS

WITH MAX AXIOM SUPER SCIENTIST

An Augmented Reading Science Experience

Fountaindale Public Library
Bolingbrook, IL
(630) 759-2102

by Agnieszka Biskup | illustrated by Tod Smith

Consultant:
Dr. Ronald Browne, Associate Professor of Elementary Education
Minnesota State University, Mankato

CAPSTONE PRESS
a capstone imprint

Graphic Library is published by Capstone Press,
1710 Roe Crest Drive, North Mankato, Minnesota 56003.
www.mycapstone.com

Library of Congress Cataloging-in-Publication Data is available on the Library of
Congress website.
ISBN: 978-1-5435-2946-3 (library binding)
ISBN: 978-1-5435-2957-9 (paperback)
ISBN: 978-1-5435-2967-8 (eBook PDF)

Summary: In graphic novel format, follows the adventures of Max Axiom as he
explains the science behind ecosystems.

Art Director and Designer
Bob Lentz and Thomas Emery

Colorist
Matt Webb

Cover Artist
Tod Smith

Editor
Donald Lemke

Photo Credits
Capstone Studio/Karon Dubke: 29; Corel: 17

Download the Capstone 4D app!

• Ask an adult to download the Capstone 4D app.

• Scan the cover and stars inside the book for additional content.

When you scan a spread, you'll find fun extra stuff
to go with this book! You can also find these things
on the web at www.capstone4D.com using the
password: ecosystem.29463

Printed in the United States of America.

TABLE OF CONTENTS

SECTION 1

COMMUNITIES OF EARTH 4

SECTION 2

ENERGY FOR THE PLANET 10

SECTION 3

WORLD'S BIOMES 20

SECTION 4

A DELICATE BALANCE 24

More About Ecosystems 28
Terrarium Time! 29
Discussion Questions, Writing Prompts, Take a Quiz! 30
Glossary 31
Read More, Internet Sites, Index 32

SECTION 1 COMMUNITIES OF EARTH

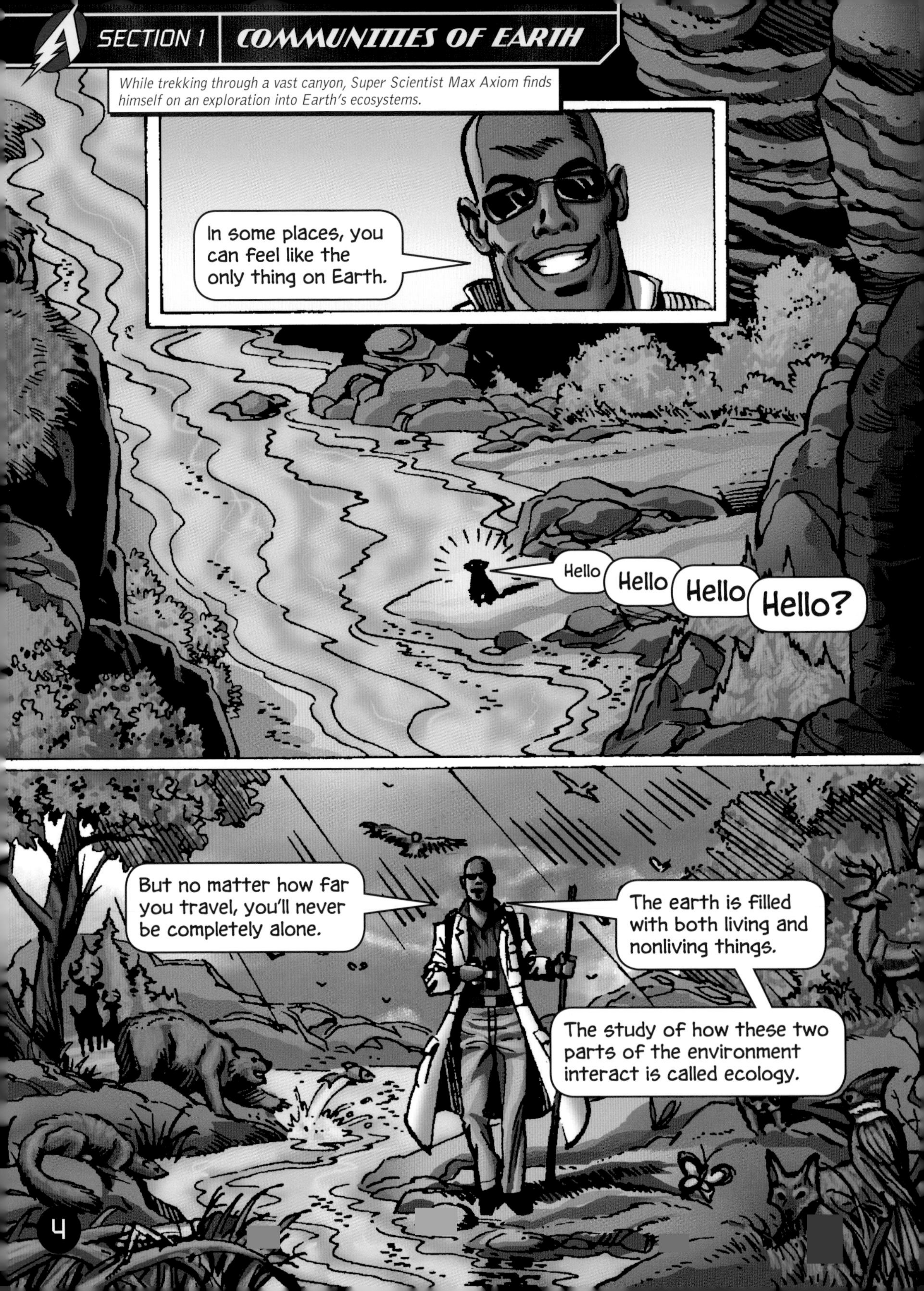
While trekking through a vast canyon, Super Scientist Max Axiom finds himself on an exploration into Earth's ecosystems.
In some places, you can feel like the only thing on Earth.
Hello
Hello
Hello
Hello?
But no matter how far you travel, you'll never be completely alone.
The earth is filled with both living and nonliving things.
The study of how these two parts of the environment interact is called ecology.

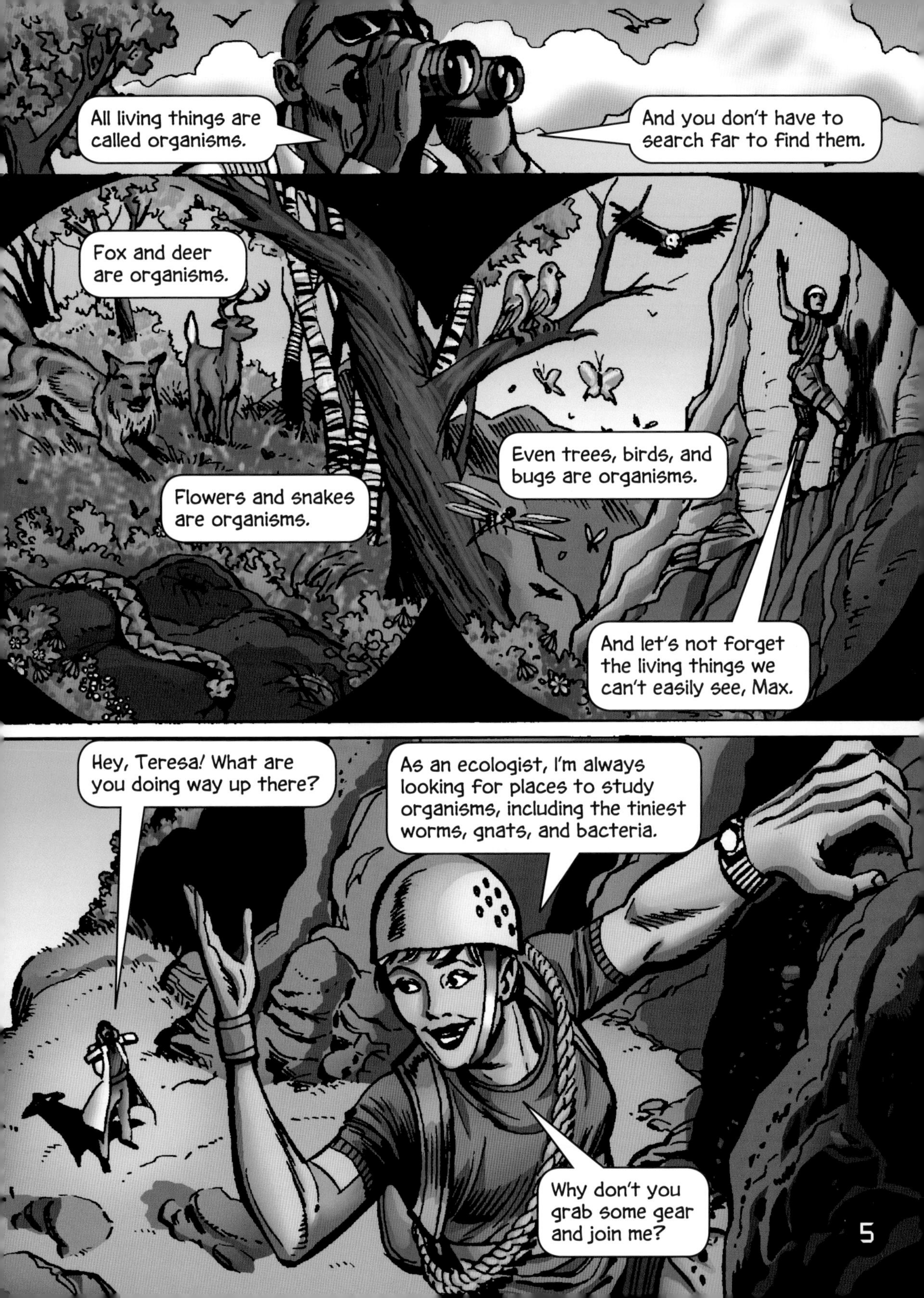
All living things are called organisms.
And you don't have to search far to find them.
Fox and deer are organisms.
Flowers and snakes are organisms.
Even trees, birds, and bugs are organisms.
And let's not forget the living things we can't easily see, Max.
Hey, Teresa! What are you doing way up there?
As an ecologist, I'm always looking for places to study organisms, including the tiniest worms, gnats, and bacteria.
Why don't you grab some gear and join me?

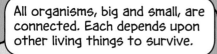

All organisms, big and small, are connected. Each depends upon other living things to survive.

That's right, Max! Many animals eat plants for energy to live.

Some survive by eating other animals.

The earth is also full of things that aren't alive.

And not just when they're dangling from a cliff! Right, Teresa?

Like sunlight, which gives plants energy to make food.

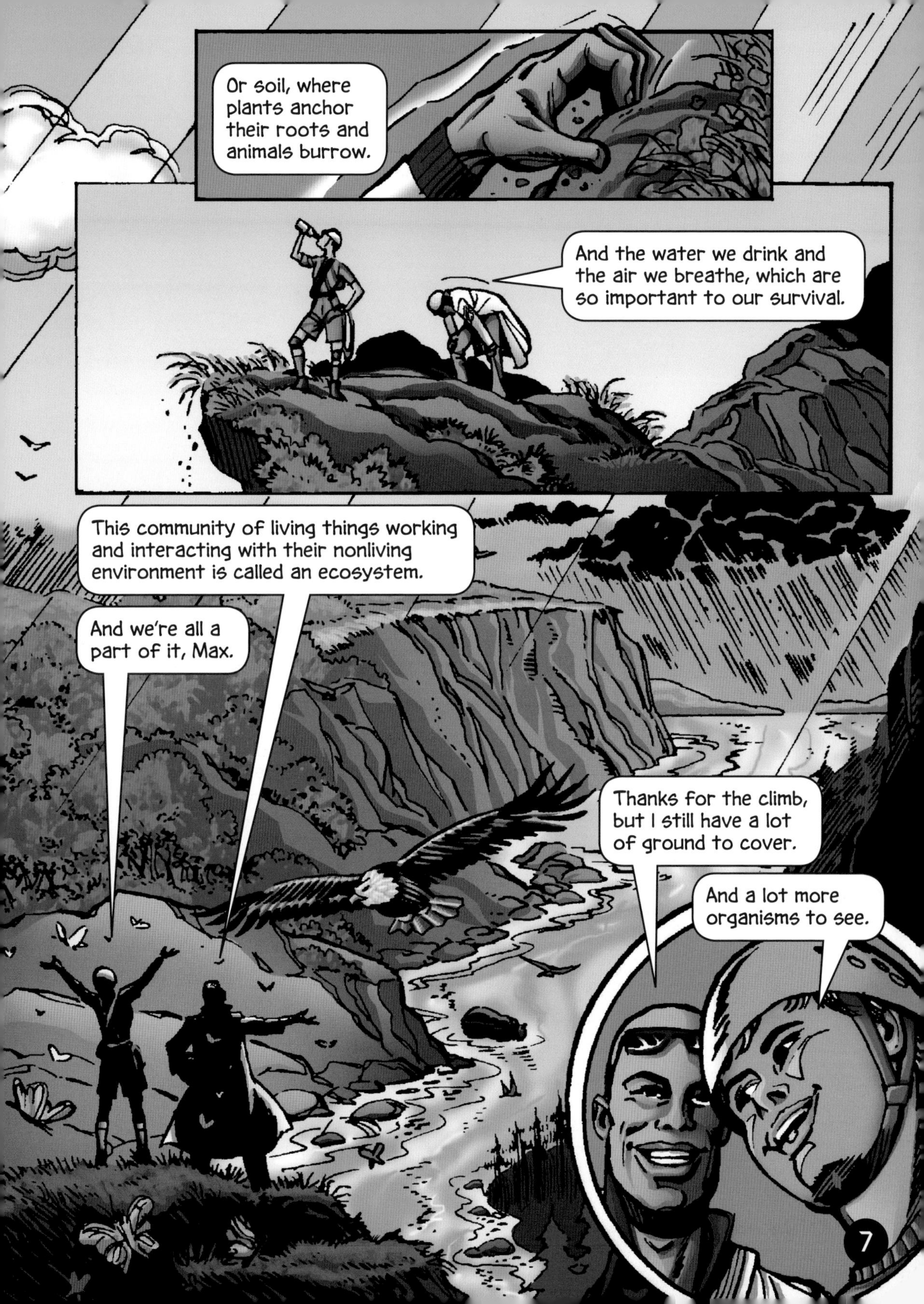
Or soil, where plants anchor their roots and animals burrow.
And the water we drink and the air we breathe, which are so important to our survival.
This community of living things working and interacting with their nonliving environment is called an ecosystem.
And we're all a part of it, Max.
Thanks for the climb, but I still have a lot of ground to cover.
And a lot more organisms to see.

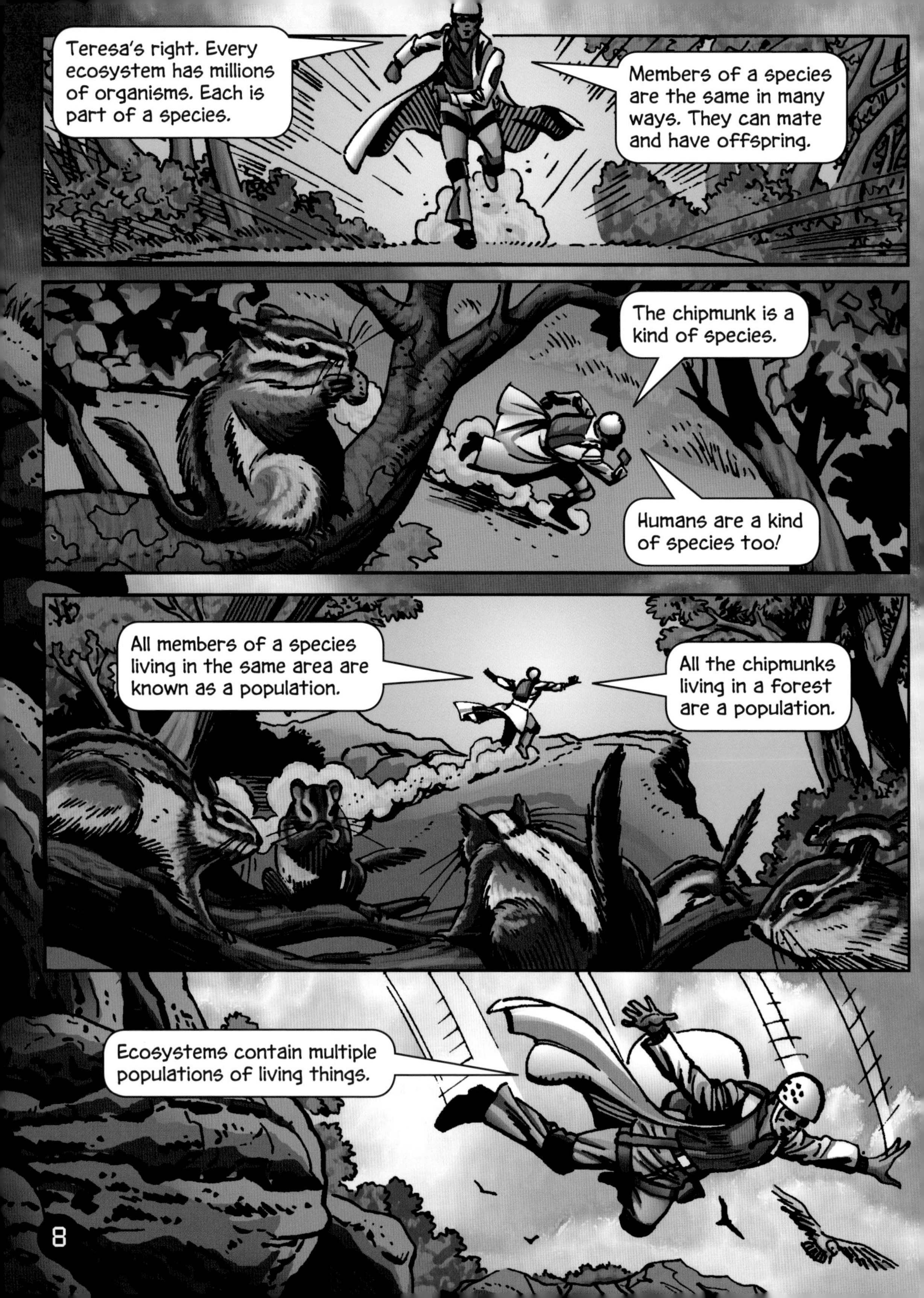

Teresa's right. Every ecosystem has millions of organisms. Each is part of a species.
Members of a species are the same in many ways. They can mate and have offspring.
The chipmunk is a kind of species.
Humans are a kind of species too!
All members of a species living in the same area are known as a population.
All the chipmunks living in a forest are a population.
Ecosystems contain multiple populations of living things.

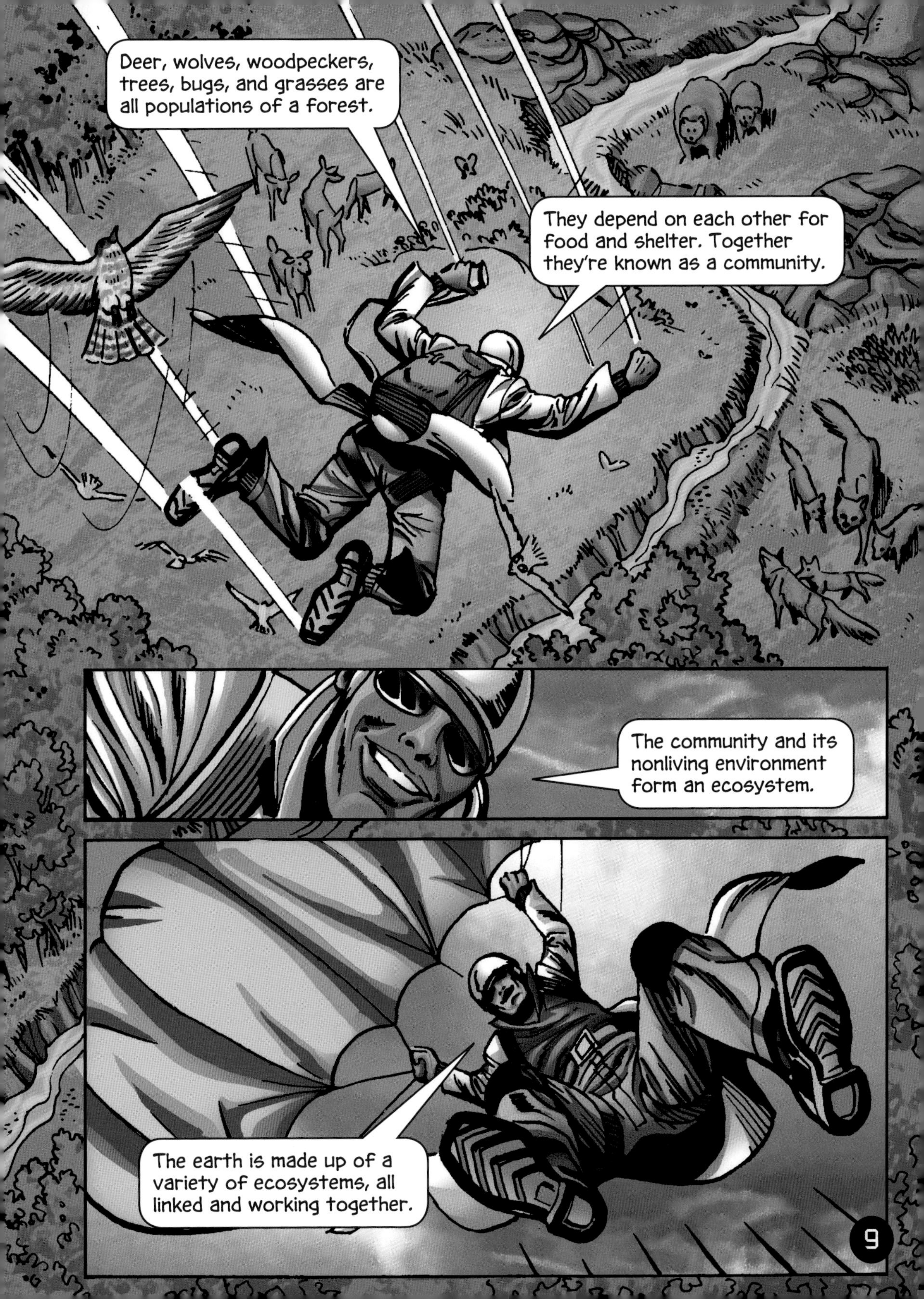
Deer, wolves, woodpeckers, trees, bugs, and grasses are all populations of a forest.
They depend on each other for food and shelter. Together they're known as a community.
The community and its nonliving environment form an ecosystem.
The earth is made up of a variety of ecosystems, all linked and working together.

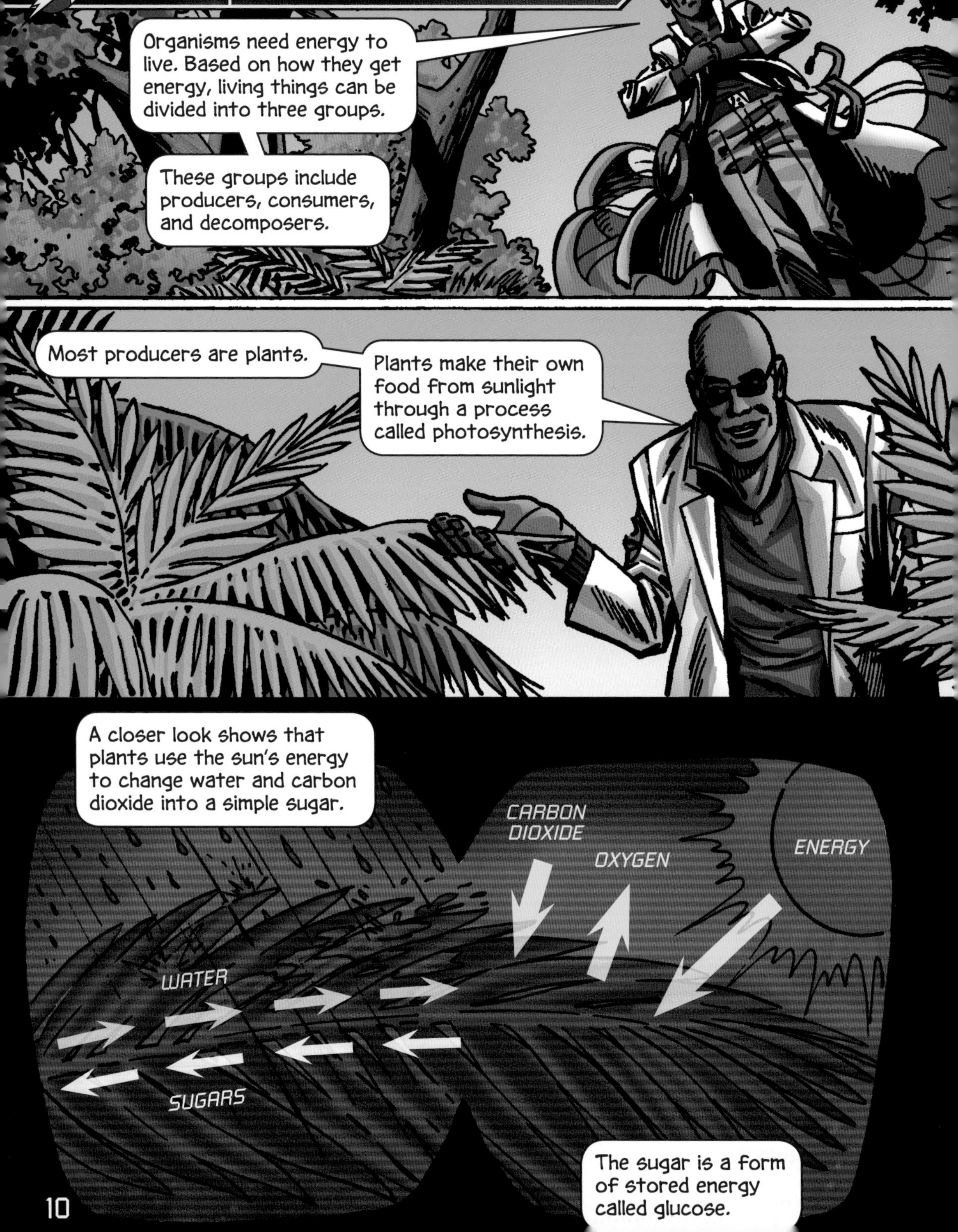
Organisms need energy to live. Based on how they get energy, living things can be divided into three groups.
These groups include producers, consumers, and decomposers.
Most producers are plants.
Plants make their own food from sunlight through a process called photosynthesis.
A closer look shows that plants use the sun's energy to change water and carbon dioxide into a simple sugar.
CARBON DIOXIDE
OXYGEN
ENERGY
WATER
SUGARS
The sugar is a form of stored energy called glucose.

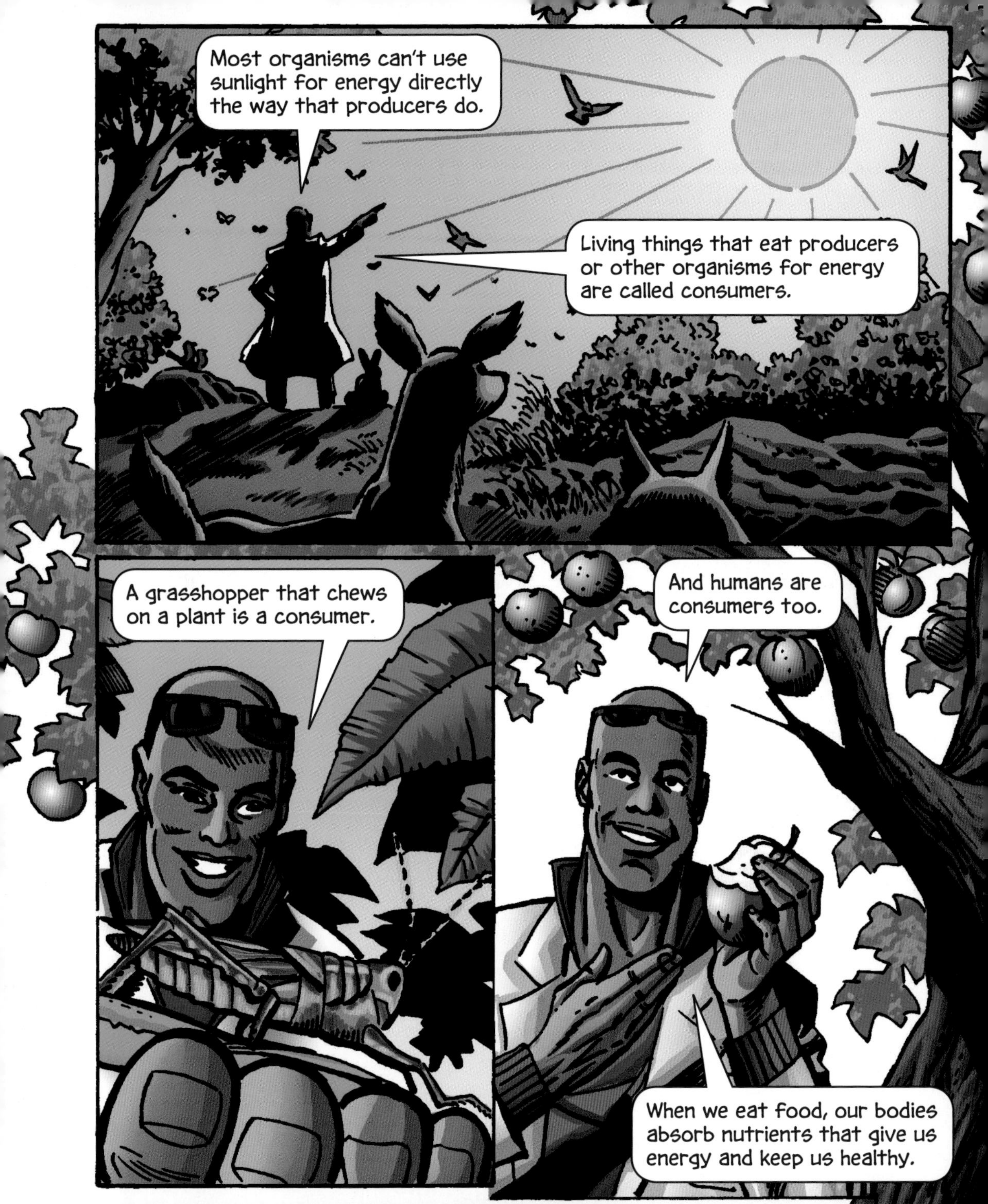
Most organisms can't use sunlight for energy directly the way that producers do.
Living things that eat producers or other organisms for energy are called consumers.
A grasshopper that chews on a plant is a consumer.
And humans are consumers too.
When we eat food, our bodies absorb nutrients that give us energy and keep us healthy.

DEFINITION

nutrient (NOO-tree-uhnt)—a substance needed by a living thing to stay healthy; plants get nutrients mainly from the soil in the form of minerals; animals get nutrients mainly from the foods they eat.

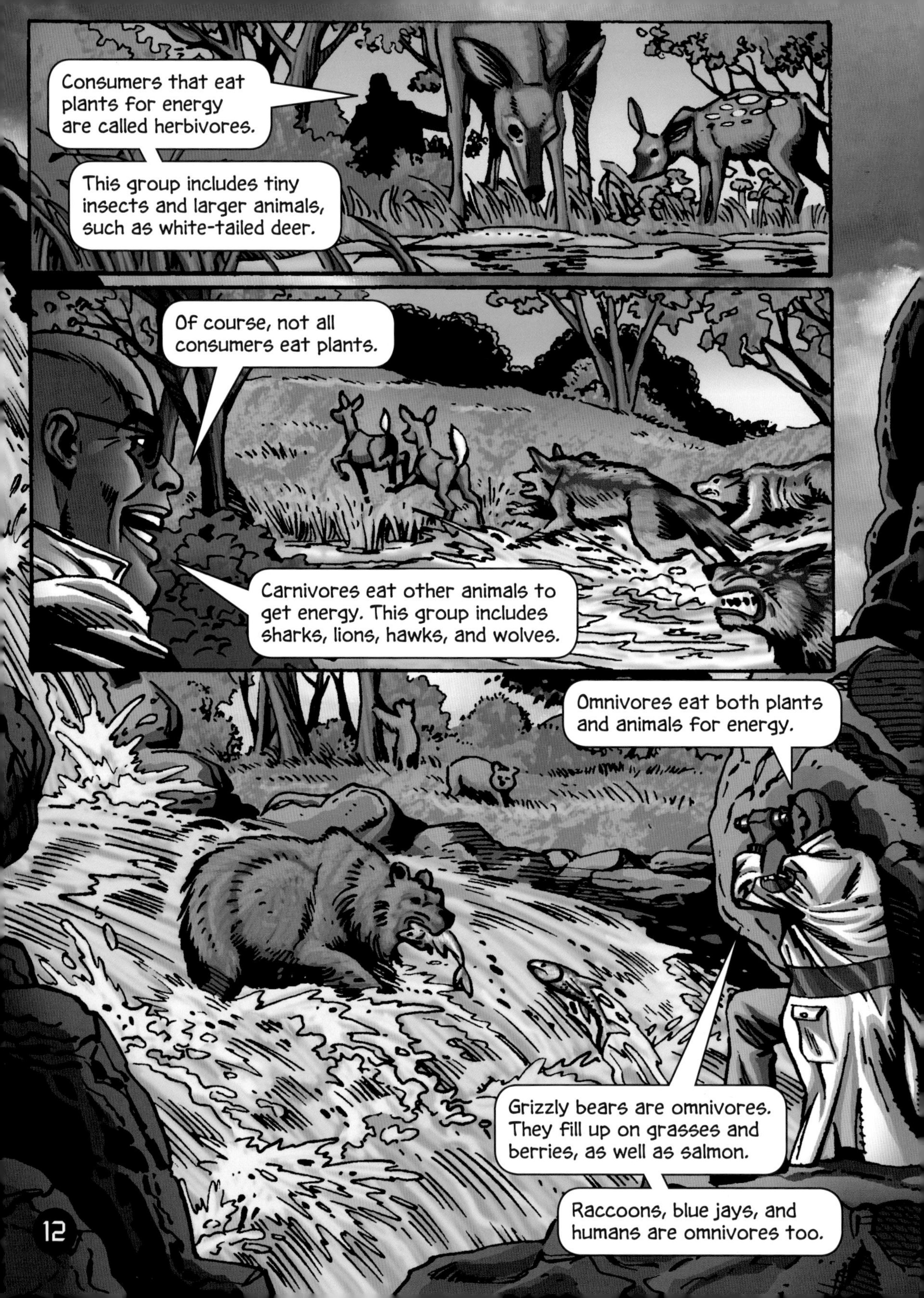
Consumers that eat plants for energy are called herbivores.
This group includes tiny insects and larger animals, such as white-tailed deer.
Of course, not all consumers eat plants.
Carnivores eat other animals to get energy. This group includes sharks, lions, hawks, and wolves.
Omnivores eat both plants and animals for energy.
Grizzly bears are omnivores. They fill up on grasses and berries, as well as salmon.
Raccoons, blue jays, and humans are omnivores too.

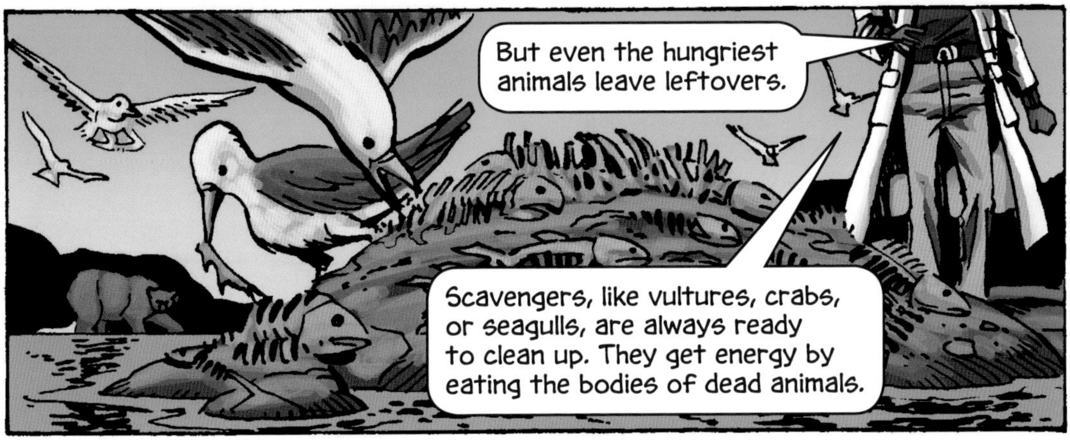
But even the hungriest animals leave leftovers.
Scavengers, like vultures, crabs, or seagulls, are always ready to clean up. They get energy by eating the bodies of dead animals.

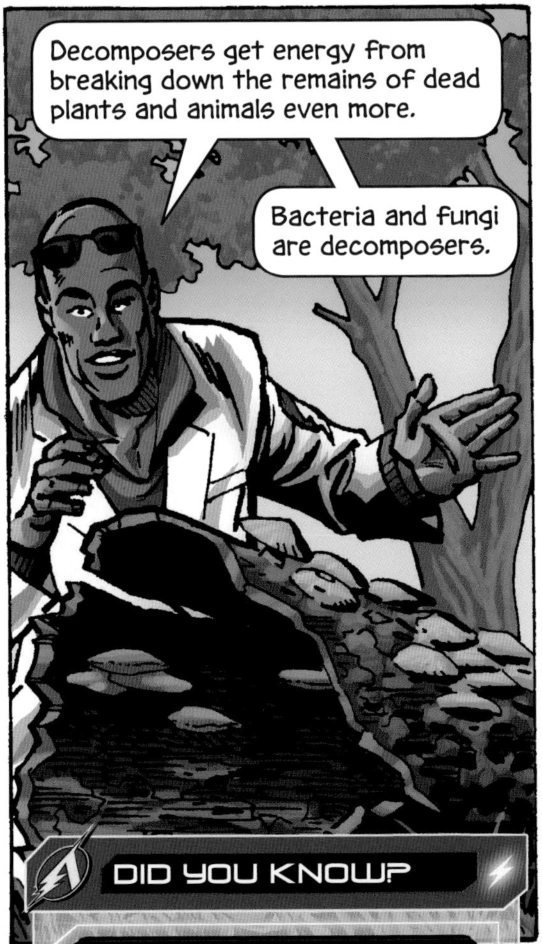
Decomposers get energy from breaking down the remains of dead plants and animals even more.
Bacteria and fungi are decomposers.

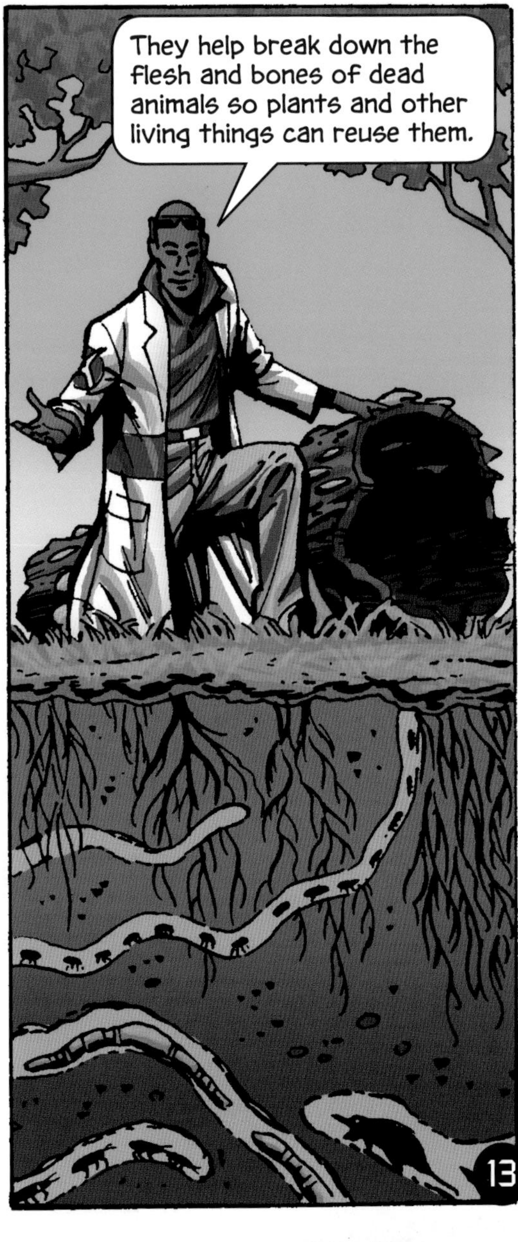
They help break down the flesh and bones of dead animals so plants and other living things can reuse them.

DID YOU KNOW?

Without decomposers and scavengers, the world would be full of the remains of dead plants and animals. As nature's recyclers, decomposers are a necessary part of an ecosystem.

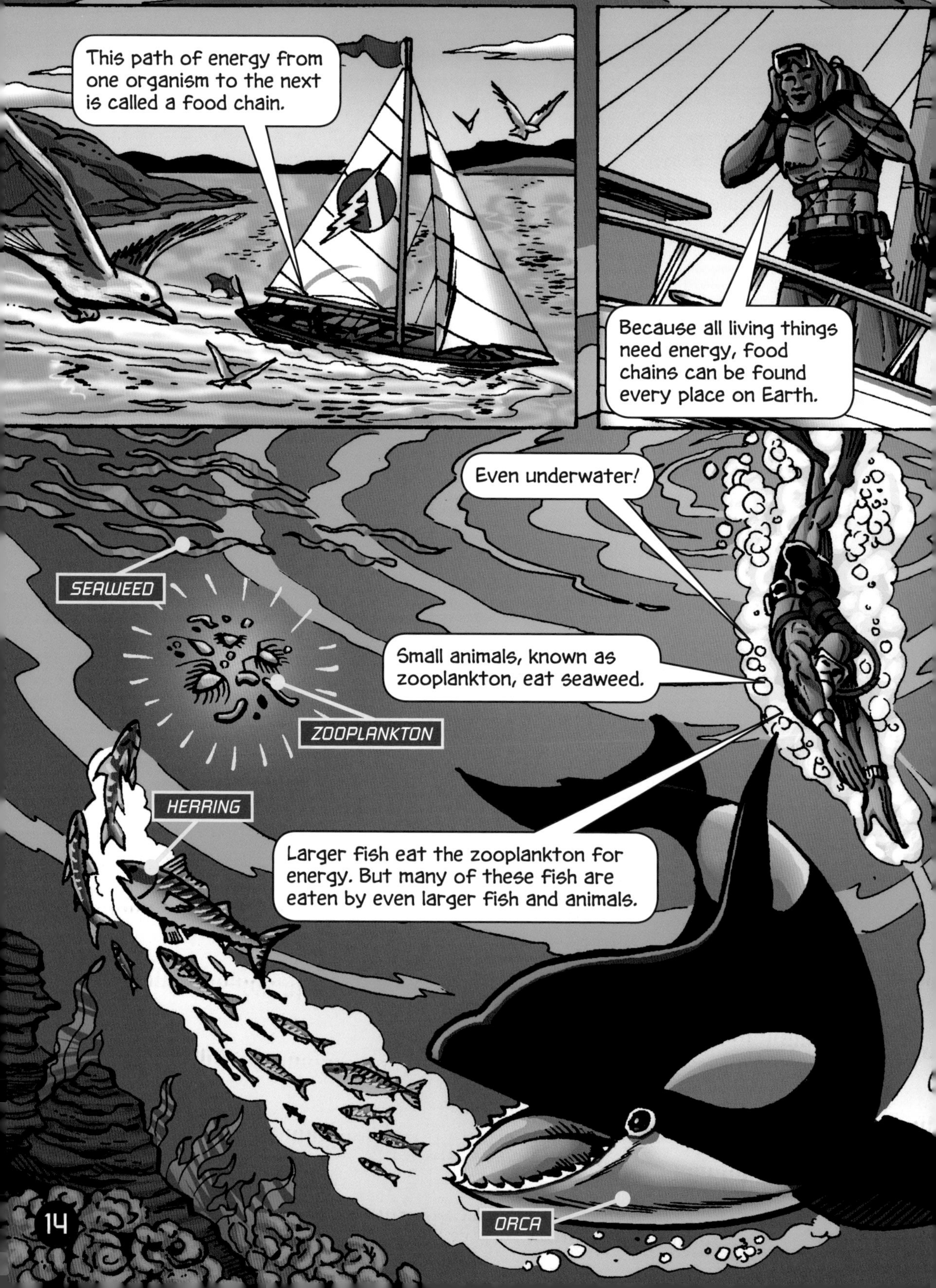
This path of energy from one organism to the next is called a food chain.
Because all living things need energy, food chains can be found every place on Earth.
Even underwater!
SEAWEED
Small animals, known as zooplankton, eat seaweed.
ZOOPLANKTON
HERRING
Larger fish eat the zooplankton for energy. But many of these fish are eaten by even larger fish and animals.
ORCA

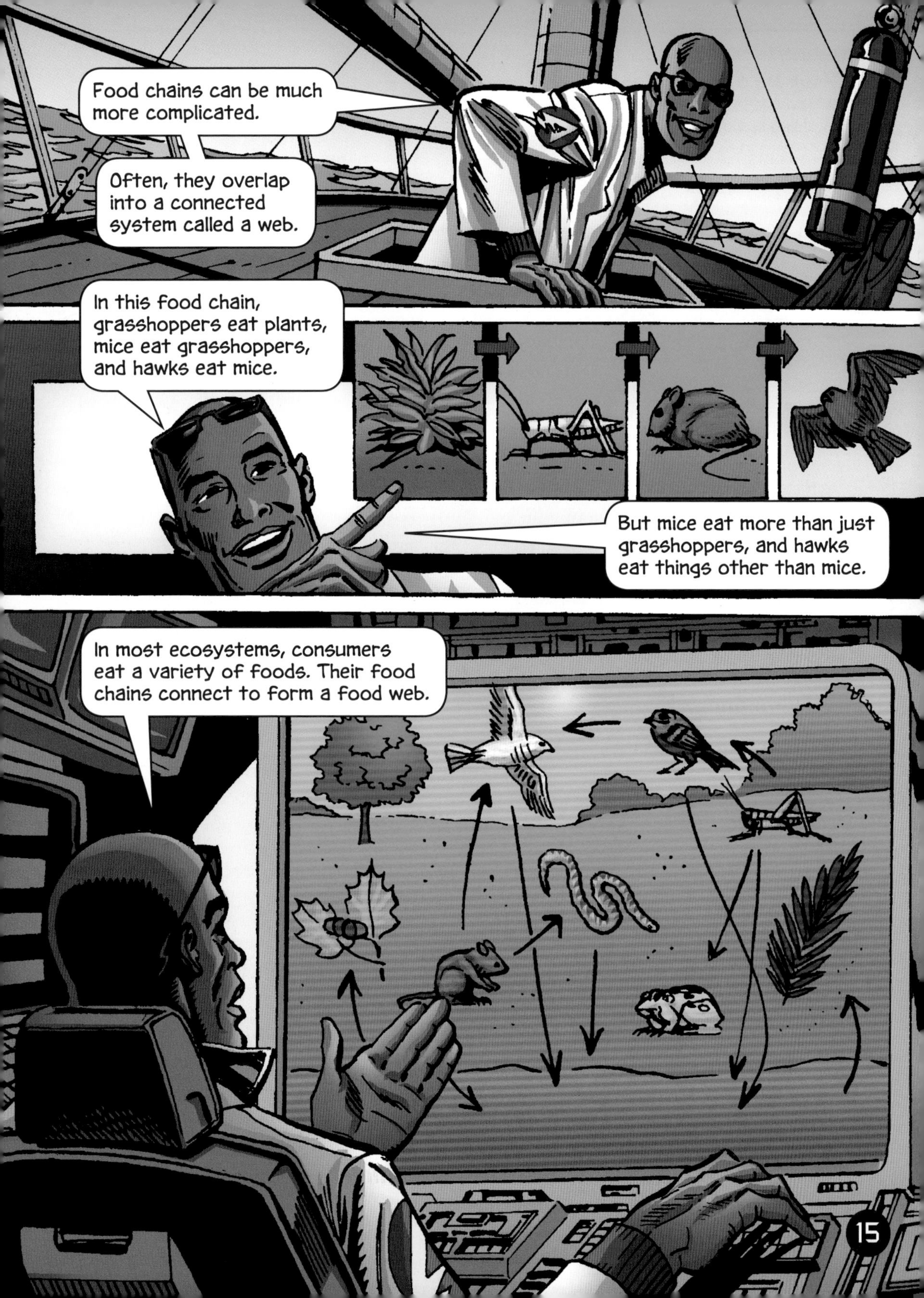
Food chains can be much more complicated.
Often, they overlap into a connected system called a web.
In this food chain, grasshoppers eat plants, mice eat grasshoppers, and hawks eat mice.
But mice eat more than just grasshoppers, and hawks eat things other than mice.
In most ecosystems, consumers eat a variety of foods. Their food chains connect to form a food web.

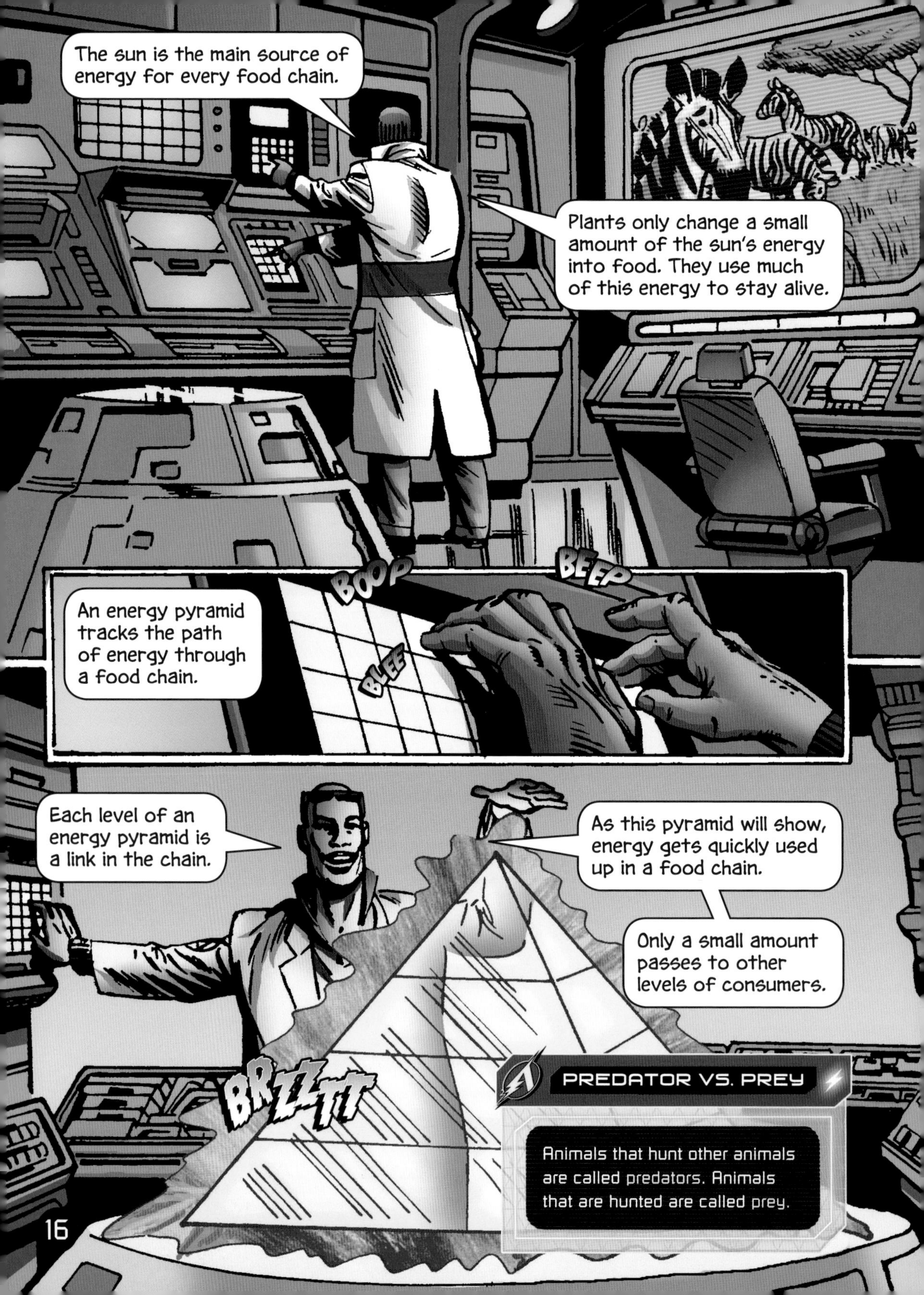
The sun is the main source of energy for every food chain.
Plants only change a small amount of the sun's energy into food. They use much of this energy to stay alive.
BOOP
BEEP
An energy pyramid tracks the path of energy through a food chain.
BLEE
Each level of an energy pyramid is a link in the chain.
As this pyramid will show, energy gets quickly used up in a food chain.
Only a small amount passes to other levels of consumers.
BRZZTT

PREDATOR VS. PREY

Animals that hunt other animals are called predators. Animals that are hunted are called prey.

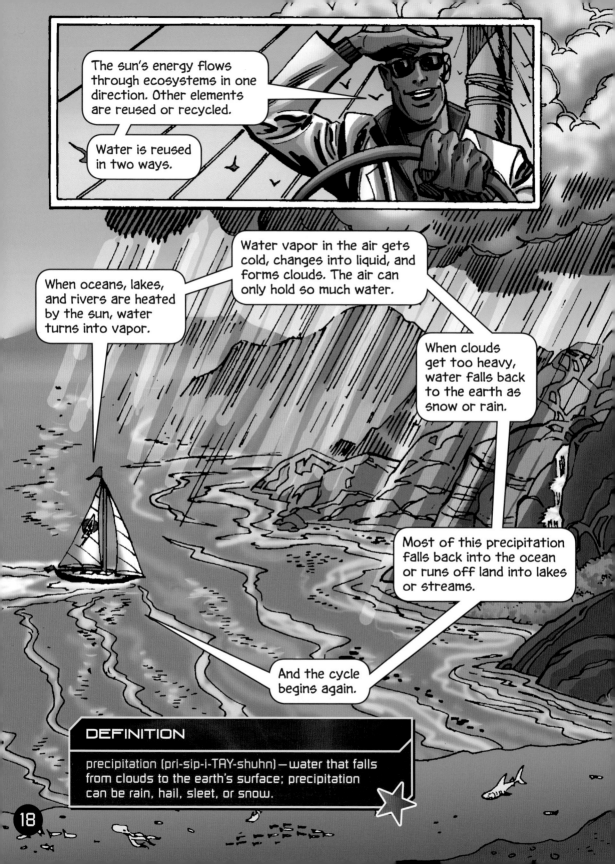

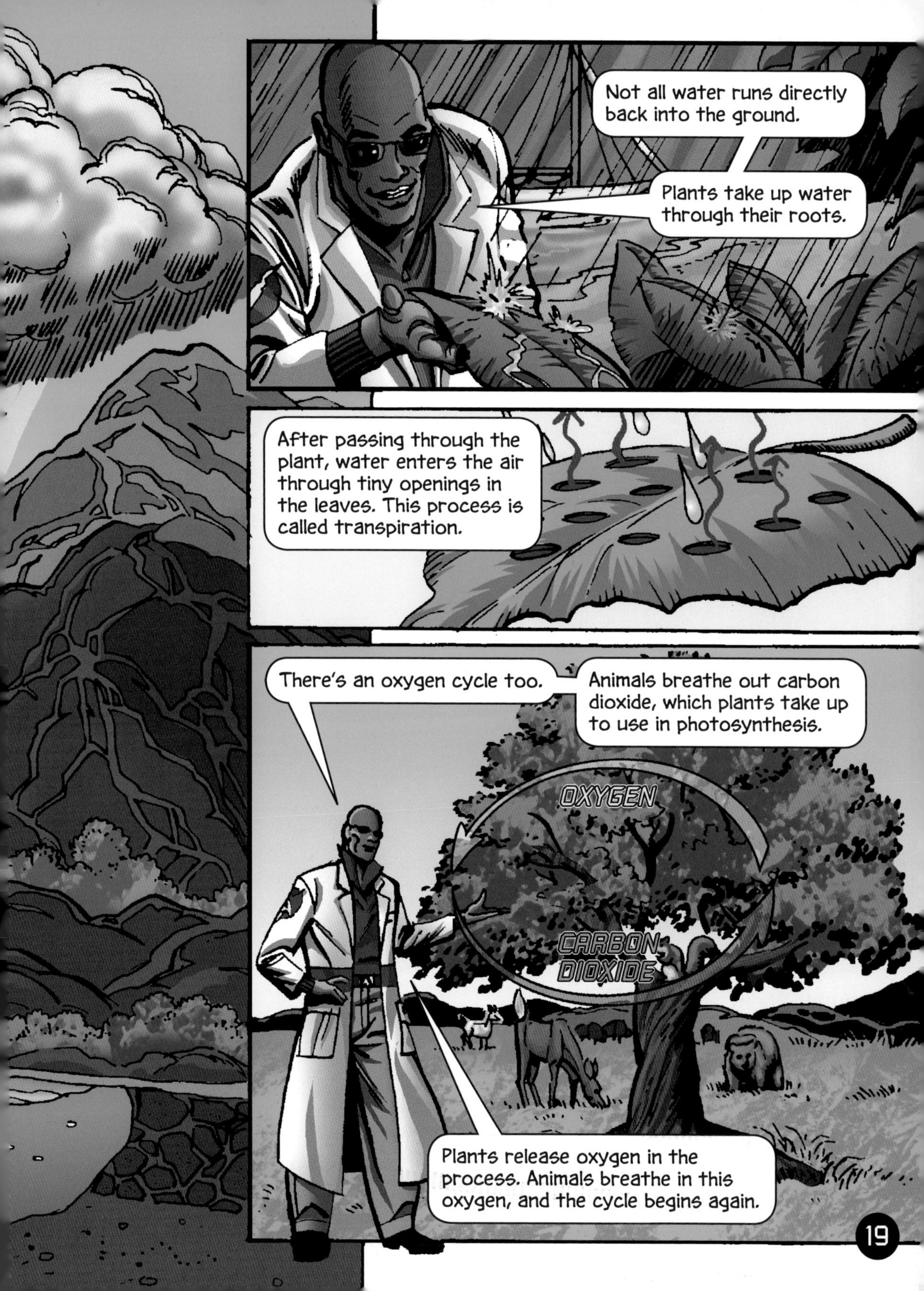

Not all water runs directly back into the ground.
Plants take up water through their roots.
After passing through the plant, water enters the air through tiny openings in the leaves. This process is called transpiration.
There's an oxygen cycle too.
Animals breathe out carbon dioxide, which plants take up to use in photosynthesis.
OXYGEN
CARBON DIOXIDE
Plants release oxygen in the process. Animals breathe in this oxygen, and the cycle begins again.

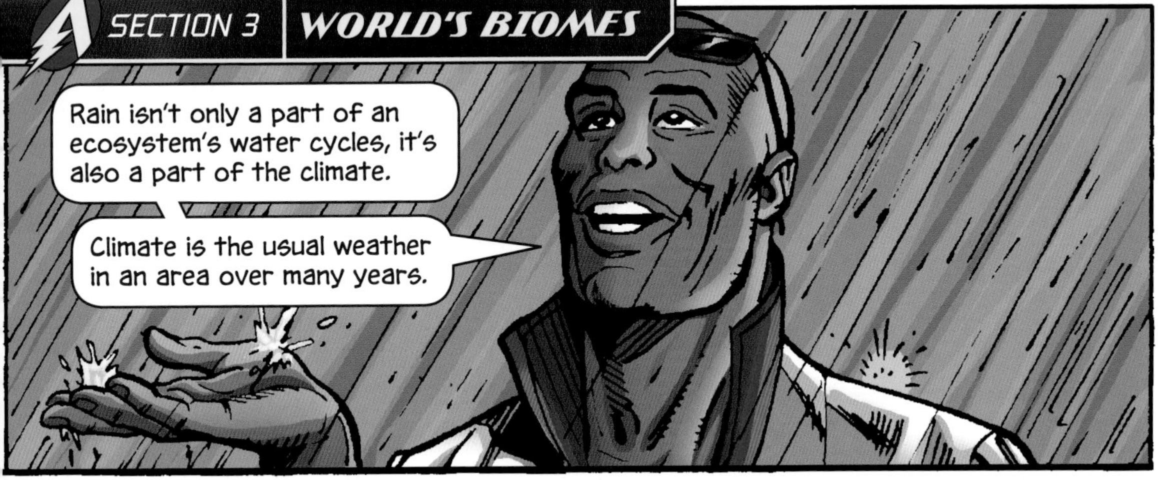
Rain isn't only a part of an ecosystem's water cycles, it's also a part of the climate.
Climate is the usual weather in an area over many years.

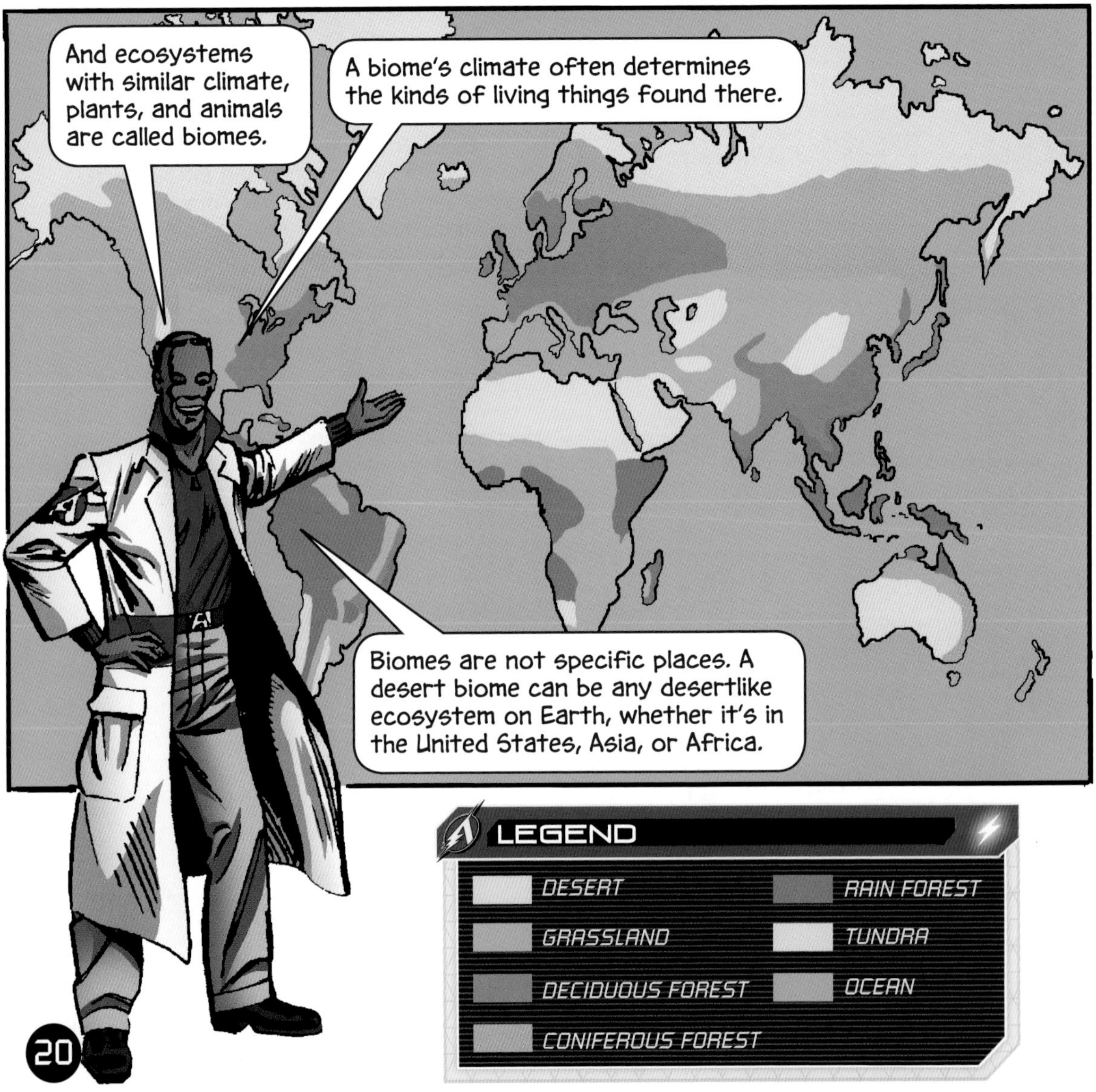
And ecosystems with similar climate, plants, and animals are called biomes.
A biome's climate often determines the kinds of living things found there.
Biomes are not specific places. A desert biome can be any desertlike ecosystem on Earth, whether it's in the United States, Asia, or Africa.
LEGEND
DESERT
GRASSLAND
DECIDUOUS FOREST
CONIFEROUS FOREST
RAIN FOREST
TUNDRA
OCEAN

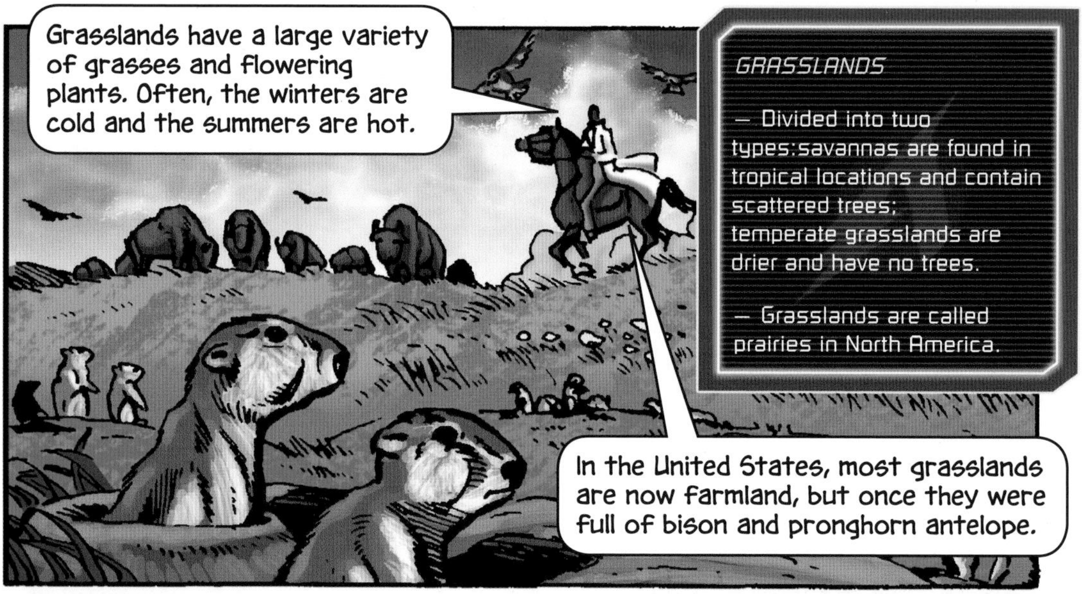
Grasslands have a large variety of grasses and flowering plants. Often, the winters are cold and the summers are hot.
GRASSLANDS
— Divided into two types:savannas are found in tropical locations and contain scattered trees; temperate grasslands are drier and have no trees.
— Grasslands are called prairies in North America.
In the United States, most grasslands are now farmland, but once they were full of bison and pronghorn antelope.

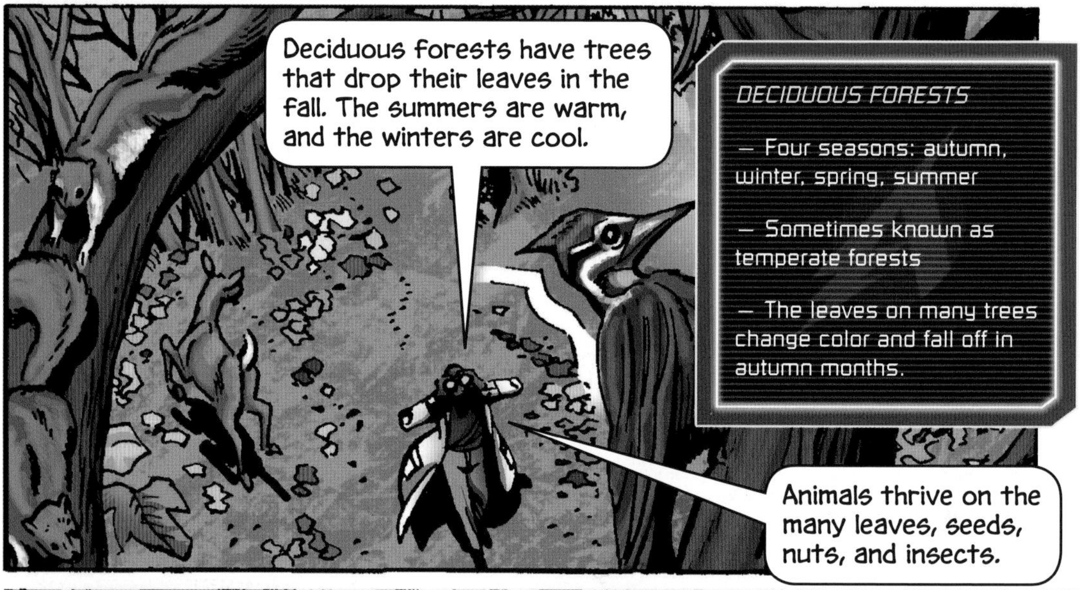
Deciduous forests have trees that drop their leaves in the fall. The summers are warm, and the winters are cool.
DECIDUOUS FORESTS
— Four seasons: autumn, winter, spring, summer
— Sometimes known as temperate forests
— The leaves on many trees change color and fall off in autumn months.
Animals thrive on the many leaves, seeds, nuts, and insects.

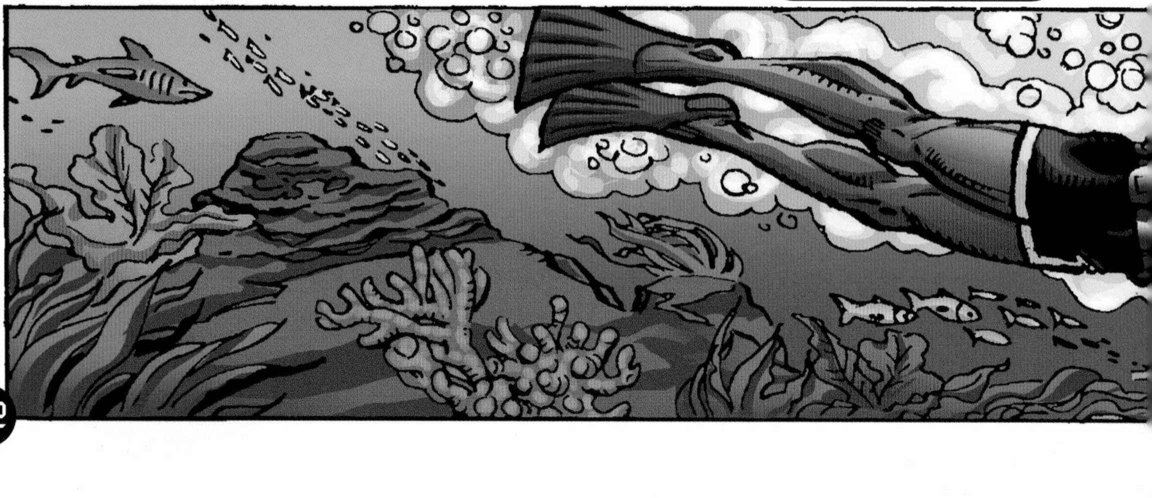

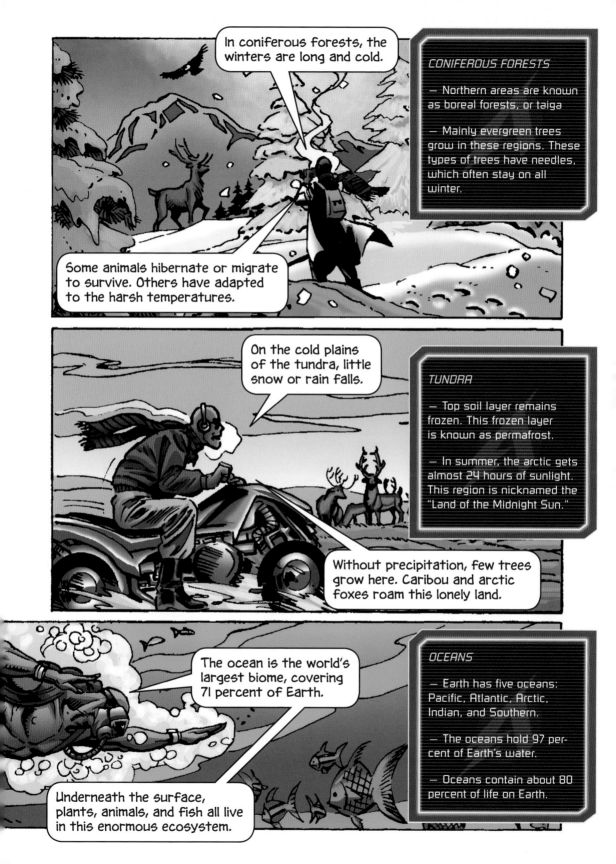

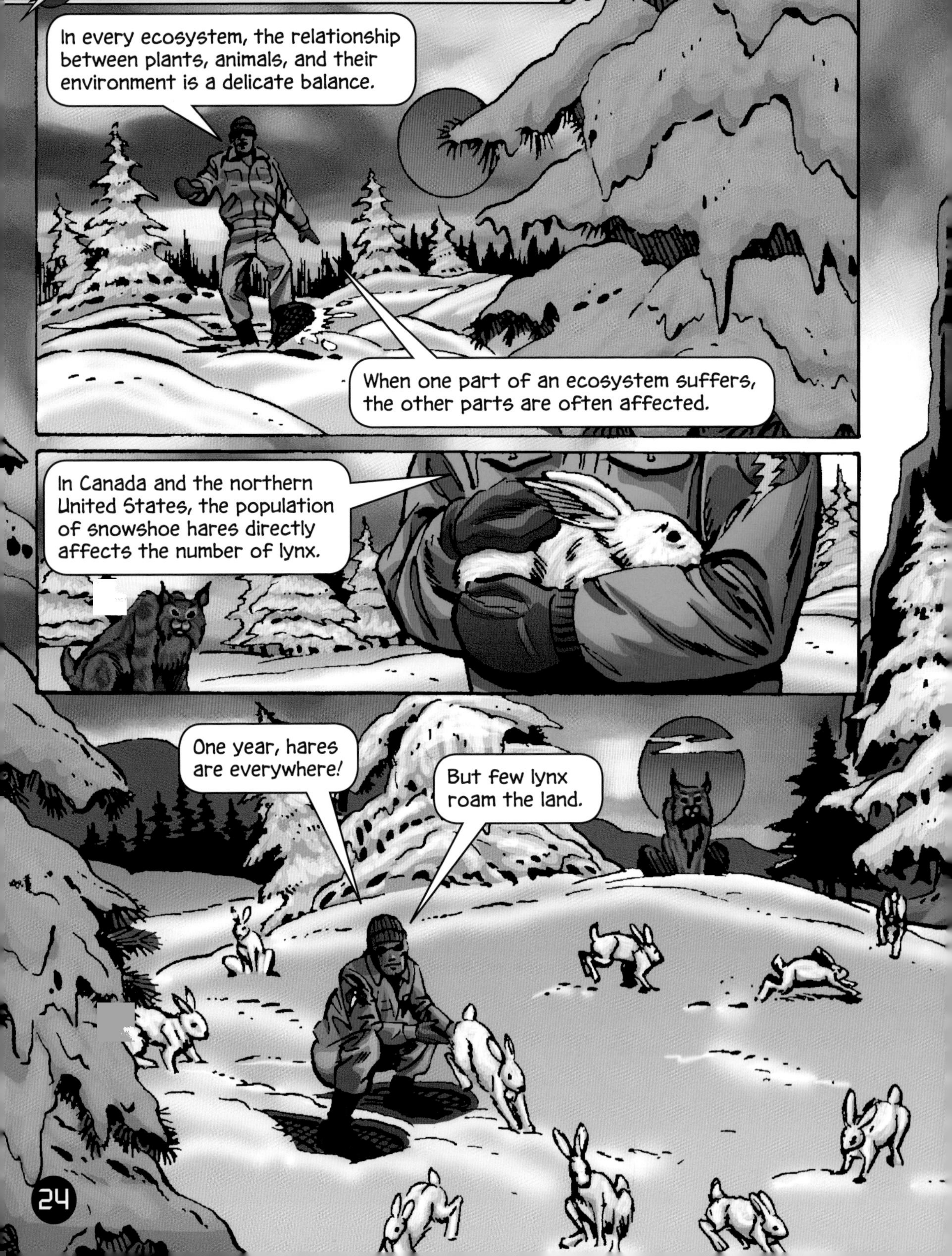
In every ecosystem, the relationship between plants, animals, and their environment is a delicate balance.
When one part of an ecosystem suffers, the other parts are often affected.
In Canada and the northern United States, the population of snowshoe hares directly affects the number of lynx.
One year, hares are everywhere!
But few lynx roam the land.

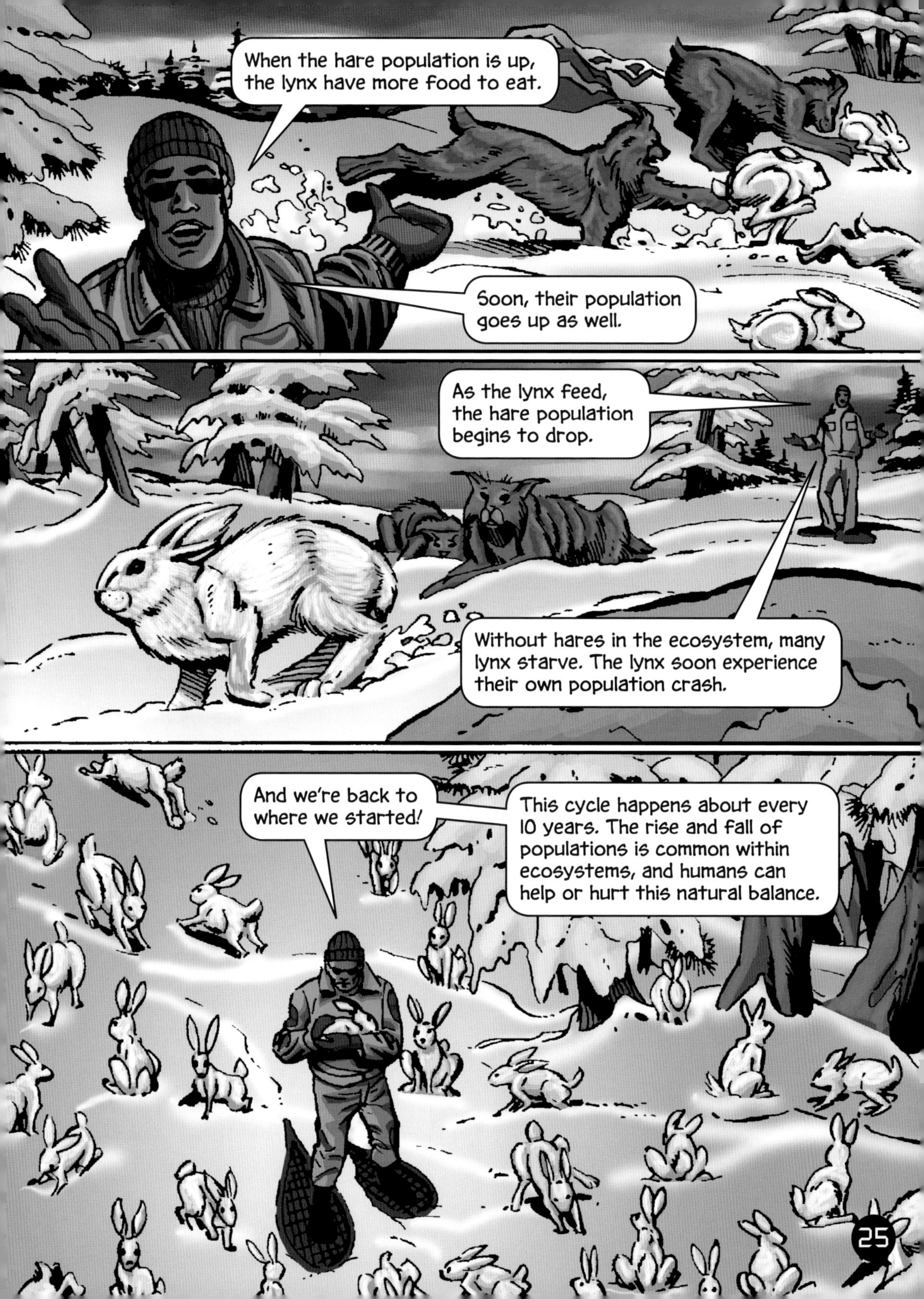
When the hare population is up, the lynx have more food to eat.
Soon, their population goes up as well.
As the lynx feed, the hare population begins to drop.
Without hares in the ecosystem, many lynx starve. The lynx soon experience their own population crash.
And we're back to where we started!
This cycle happens about every 10 years. The rise and fall of populations is common within ecosystems, and humans can help or hurt this natural balance.

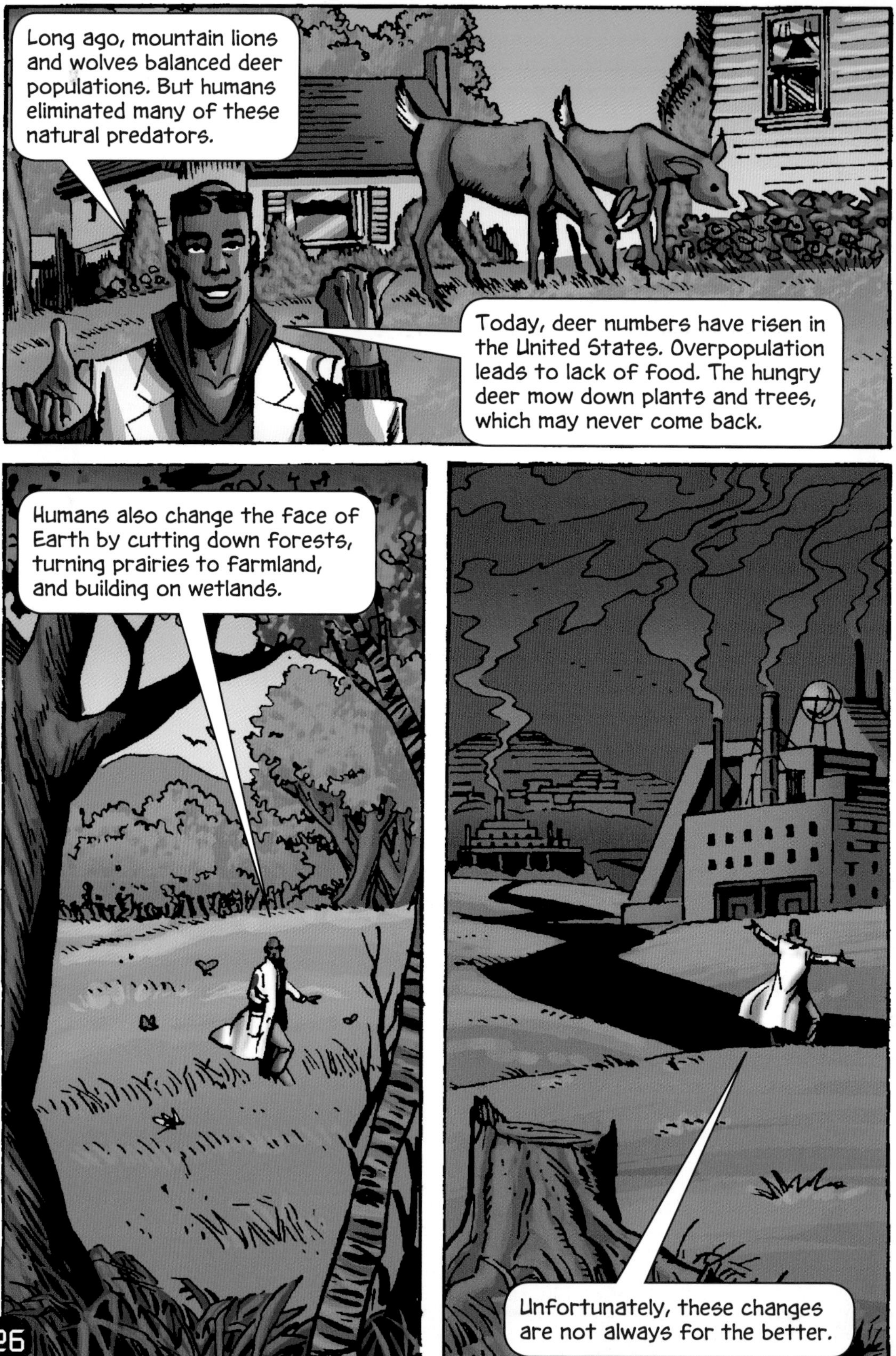
Long ago, mountain lions and wolves balanced deer populations. But humans eliminated many of these natural predators.
Today, deer numbers have risen in the United States. Overpopulation leads to lack of food. The hungry deer mow down plants and trees, which may never come back.
Humans also change the face of Earth by cutting down forests, turning prairies to farmland, and building on wetlands.
Unfortunately, these changes are not always for the better.

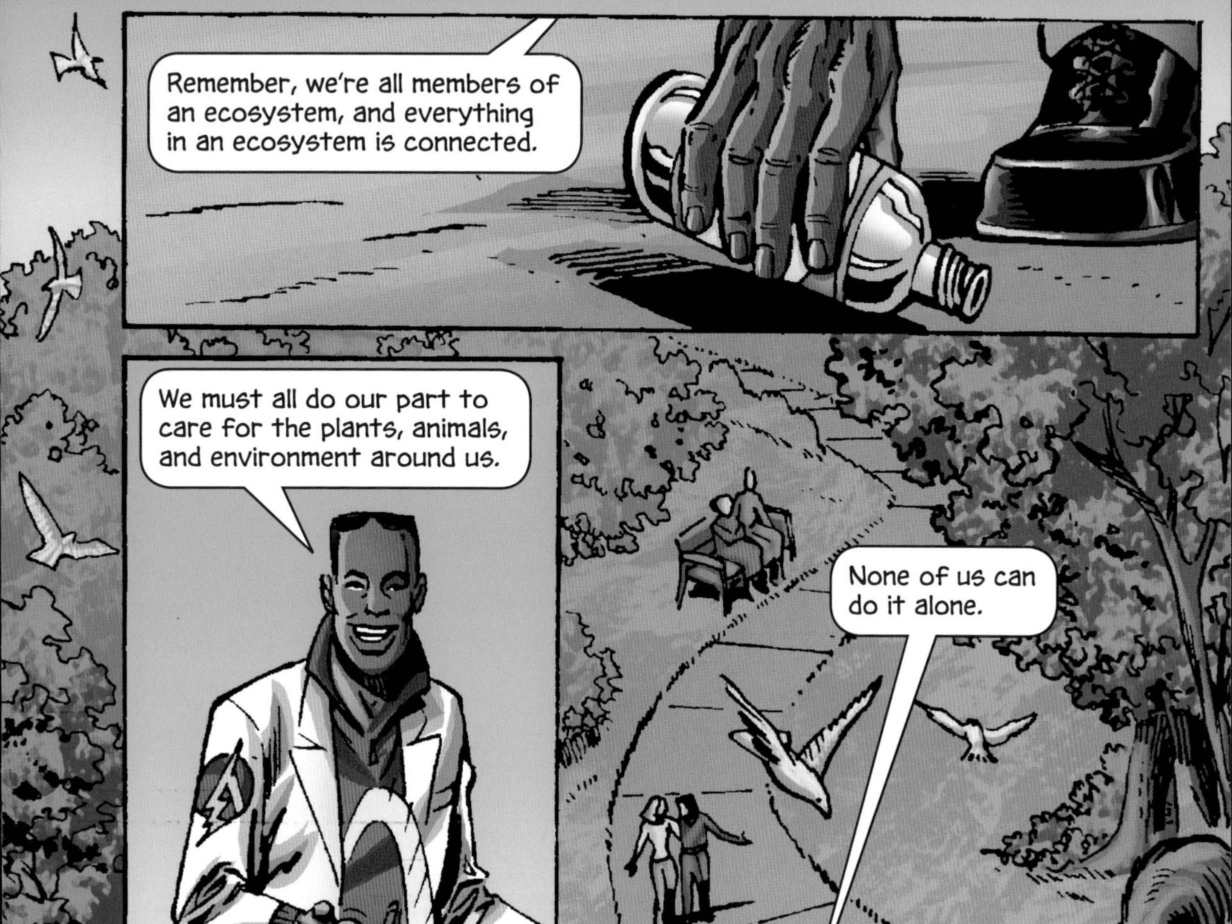
Remember, we're all members of an ecosystem, and everything in an ecosystem is connected.
We must all do our part to care for the plants, animals, and environment around us.
RECYCLE
None of us can do it alone.

REDUCE YOUR IMPACT

You can protect the earth's ecosystems by practicing conservation. Use fewer natural resources like water and gas. Reduce waste and pollution whenever possible. Recycle bottles, cans, paper, and other recyclable materials.

Ecosystems can be as large as an ocean or as small as a fishbowl. To identify the many ecosystems, some are named after their main feature, such as a pond ecosystem, a salt marsh ecosystem, or a redwood forest ecosystem.

Ecosystems are fragile, and alien invasive species can be a major problem. These plants and animals have been introduced to a part of the world where they don't belong. The brown tree snake was originally from Australia and Indonesia. Somehow, this sneaky reptile slithered onto a plane and hitched a ride to the island of Guam. With few predators on Guam, the tree snake has nearly wiped out native forest birds.

Believe it or not, the extinct passenger pigeon was once among the most numerous animals on earth. In the early 1800s, the passenger pigeon population was estimated at 1 to 5 billion birds. Huge, migrating flocks actually darkened the sky when they passed. Largely due to overhunting, the pigeons began to decline. By the 1890s, only small flocks were left. The last passenger pigeon, named Martha, died in the Cincinnati Zoo in 1914.

In the early 1990s, scientists tried to reproduce the ecosystems of earth inside a 3.5-acre (1.4-hectare) building called Biosphere 2. Located near Tucson, Arizona, the building contained a desert, a rain forest, and even a 900,000-gallon (3,406,860-liter) ocean. Some scientists believed buildings like Biosphere 2 could support life on the Moon or Mars. But after only two disappointing missions inside, the experiments ended. Today, visitors can tour the building and learn more about Earth's fragile ecosystems.

The rain forest is one of the largest biomes on earth. Sadly, more than 1.5 acres (.6 hectare) of rain forest are destroyed every second.

TERRARIUM TIME!

Turn a plain glass jar into a biosphere bursting with life! With its balance of light, water, air, and plants, a terrarium is a little ecosystem all its own.

WHAT YOU NEED:

- glass jar with a lid
- ruler
- small pebbles
- sand
- activated charcoal (found at most pet stores)

- potting soil
- small plants
- live mosssticks or stones
- small toy plants or animals
- water

WHAT YOU DO:

1. Thoroughly clean and dry the jar. The jar needs to be very clean to avoid any mold growth.

2. Add a 1-inch (2.5 centimeter) layer of clean sand to the bottom of the jar.

3. Add a 1-inch (2.5 cm) layer of pebbles on top of the sand. These layers will create a water basin for your ecosystem.

4. Add a ½-inch (1.25 cm) layer of activated charcoal on top of the sand. This layer will act as a filter to keep your ecosystem clean.

5. Add a 2-inch (5 cm) layer of well-draining potting soil.

6. Plant small plants and moss in the soil. Make sure to cover the roots fully. Small, slow-growing plants and moss that can handle warm, humid, environments work best.

7. Add decorative items you like—maybe a neat-looking piece of wood or a rock you've collected.

8. Add small toy animals and plants to represent other organisms in your ecosystem.

9. Water the terrarium so that the sand layer is wet.

10. Cap your terrarium and place it near a window, but out of direct sunlight. If condensation appears, uncap the jar for a day to allow some water to evaporate.

11. Watch as the terrarium self-regulates and cares for itself. If it becomes dry, give it just a little bit of water and move it into more indirect light.

DISCUSSION QUESTIONS

1. How have humans changed the ecosystems white-tailed deer live in? Discuss how each change has affected the deer population.

2. Plants use energy from the sun. What part of the ecosystem do they belong to and why are they important?

3. Each biome has a different climate. Which biomes get the least rain? Which biome is generally the coldest? Discuss how plants and animals have adapted to live in these biomes.

4. Wolves only eat prey they hunt on their own. What two parts of an ecosystem do wolves and their prey fall under?

WRITING PROMPTS

1. What is an ecosystem? Based on what you've read in the book, write a definition of an ecosystem in your own words.

2. Pick two of the biomes Max discusses and write a short paragraph describing the similarities and differences between them.

3. Organisms need four nonliving things in ecosystems. List these four nonliving things and draw a picture representing each one.

4. The energy pyramid tracks how energy moves through a food chain. Write what each level of the energy pyramid represents. Draw an energy pyramid with plants and animals from the area you live in.

TAKE A QUIZ!